Unbridled Messiah

Pnina Shinebourne

Published by Leaf by Leaf
an imprint of Cinnamon Press
www.cinnamonpress.com

The right of Pnina Shinebourne to be identified as author of this work has been asserted by her in accordance with the Copyright, Designs and Patent Act, 1988. © 2021, Pnina Shinebourne.
ISBN 978-1-78864-928-5

British Library Cataloguing in Publication Data. A CIP record for this book can be obtained from the British Library.

All rights reserved. No part of this publication may be reproduced, stored in a retrieval system, or transmitted in any form or by any means, electronic, mechanical, photocopying, recording or otherwise without the prior written permission of the publishers. This book may not be lent, hired out, resold or otherwise disposed of by way of trade in any form of binding or cover other than that in which it is published, without the prior consent of the publishers.

Designed and typeset in Bodoni by Cinnamon Press.
Cover design by Adam Craig © Adam Craig.
Cinnamon Press is represented by Inpress

Acknowledgements

I am grateful to Jo Shapcott, Katy Evans-Bush and members of her advanced poetry workshop for the lively discussions and searching questions, which in different ways helped to challenge my thinking and deepen my commitment to my work. Thanks are due to Anne Carson whose work has been an enduring inspiration.
Thank you, Jan Fortune for your editorial wisdom and commitment to bring this book into the world. Thanks to Alex Josephy for your meticulous editing and insightful comments. Thanks also to Adam Craig for the graceful cover design.
My deepest thanks to John, for his love, encouragement and emotional support.

Contents

Prologue	9
Dramatis Personae	9
Oddball	10
Messiah in Waiting	11
Perplexed	12
As written in the Talmud	14
Wife 1	15
Ponder	16
Wife 2	17
Spellbound	18
Abject	19
Saturn	20
Banished	21
Wife to be	22
Crashlanding	23
Maidservant	24
Wedding	25
Messiah on the edge	27
Unbridle my heart	28
Performance	29
On the road	31
Procession	32
Banquet	33
Unbeliever	34
Rage	35
Blessed	36
Messiah in love	37
A kiss	38
Miracles	39
Devotion	40
Wager	41
Soup	42
Yearning	43
Birth pangs	44
Splendid	45
Politics	47
Pilgrim	48
Gossip	49
Omen	50
Conversion	51

Obedience	53
1666	54
Wind	55
Mysteries	56
A crooked pathway	57
Betrayal	58
Miraculous	60
Postscript	62
Notes	64
Sources	65

Unbridled Messiah

Prologue

There are two of us to tell this story, like twins, often mistaken one for the other. We are the heavenly sisters, Shekinah, the divine presence of God in the world, and Lilith, a wanton demon of the night.
We sing in counterpoint, of wonder and redemption, and of demons lurking in the great abyss.
If you take a seat and listen, we'll tell you everything we know.

Dramatis Personae

Shabtai Zvi	Messiah. Native of Smyrna. Appearance beautiful and majestic. Prone to bizarre deeds.
Sarah	Messiah's wife. Renowned beauty. An angel promised her she would marry the Messiah.
Nathan	Prophet. Said to have harboured a secret attraction to Shabtai. Prophesied the messiah would be crowned in 1666, the year of the great apocalypse.
Heavenly sisters	Timeless free spirits. Hovering at low altitude. Invisible. Nosey. They hear many voices. They tell their stories.
Voices	Many.

Oddball

A bit of an oddball   wasn't he /
remember how he dressed up a
live fish as a baby and put it in
a cradle /   well you always
admire misfits don't you   Lilith
           it's hilarious you said
how it will annoy the rabbis /
    so what is he up to now /
locks himself in his room or
hides in the desert   pondering
the inner life of angels
      some days he shows up
delirious   a gaping red mouth
filled with   mood like a wide-
awake kicking baby fish /
the unquiet rustles inside him /
        do you have any idea
what it is   like   to become
a Messiah /
      not the faintest /

Messiah in Waiting

*A swirling wave dragged me down the pit of
the dark sea*, he tells mother when he comes
home all wet, hours after dinner time.

You must be starving, mother says, and puts
a fresh spinach bureka in his mouth.

He doesn't tell her he killed the fiery dragon
and the whole sea became red with blood.

*

A shudder inside his dream.
Tongues of flame lick his penis. Red scar.

A huge night spreads overhead dripping
beads of blackness into his soul.

Scar and Lilith blend in the unslept
sleep of all the years since.

And the demons of Lilith always pursue him
to lead him astray.

*

A boy in a white tunic, he dips his toes
in the sea, walks barefoot across the quayside
his mind a jumble of wonders.

He studies the Talmud and the Zohar
flush-faced
on his lips forbidden syllables
jostle for breath
a tumbledown of heaven and earth.

Splashes of demon-infested darkness
descend on his soul
on the waterfront angels hoist up a mast
sprinkle gleaming sparks over the earth.

Perplexed

Criss-crossing the desert
   in a swirl of gritty dust
      he hears God the almighty
whose voice trumpets
   from a whirlwind
      like a thunder

thou art the true messiah
   the saviour of thy people
      the voice proclaims
or so it seems
   for he is not that familiar
      with divine conversation

am I really? he asks himself
   in wonder
      for he didn't set out
to become a messiah
   didn't have a grand plan
      it just happened

he feels destined to create
   an amazing messianic performance
      but is not sure how to
like the prophet Isaiah
   he levitates to dizzy heights
      yet the people look away

unmoved
   by the live performance
      un poco loco they whisper

you are not worthy to behold
   this glorious sight he sulks
      I am *the messiah*
he cries out loud fists clenched
   free to *shake up your boring sad life*
      to speak what no mouth can utter

stop babysulking forthwith demand
older brothers who are wise
(and rich)
you bring shame on our family
be a man at once
but he doesn't know how to

and so it is back to the desert
in a swirl of gritty dust
hiding in a cave
halfway up the mountain
where God pours softly
fresh yearnings into his bones.

As written in the Talmud

In the sweaty throng of the bazaar
in the port and in the synagogues
who has not heard the latest gossip
   repeated and multiplied

>*an amazing fragrant odour radiates
>from Shabtai's body,*
>a voice whispers in my ear,
>*the smell of the Garden of Eden.*

As written in the Talmud, I told Shabtai,
*it is unbecoming for a learned young man
to go out perfumed, for it may be construed
he tries to attract other men.
What a young man needs is a wife*, I said.

I watched him strip naked for an examination
to prove there was no perfume.
It was the patriarchs, he said, *who anointed
him, but you must not reveal this mystery
until the right time.*

Wife 1

Let it fade   it was never real
the wedding was nothing more
than an apparition   his marriage vows

were just a hollow chant
and what I took to be my bridegroom
was just a man prancing.

My husband has not touched me
since the wedding
he hasn't called me by my name.

I return to my father's house
still a virgin   my hair will turn grey
I will never have a child in my belly.

Ponder

Look at him Lilith   such a
rosy-cheeked budding Messiah
clothed with the Holy Spirit /
really Shekhina   you always
see the light   but what about a
darkness in his soul   the folly
the mischief / true   sometimes
he is overdoing it   have you
heard how like Joshua he cried
out to the sun to stand still
how he uttered the ineffable
name of God   י ה ו ה /

we ponder in counterpoint /
you say
   bipolar disorder (DSM-5) /
I say
   a manic depressive saviour
   archetype (Carl Jung) /
the dictionary says
    ש ו ט ה   [shoté] – fool
    ש ו ט ה   [soté] – deviant

and we wonder how one letter
falling in and out of a word
can underscore an entire life
         how a single sound
can discern an awkward folly
from a wayward disposition.

Wife 2

Let it fade   it was never real
the wedding was nothing more
than an apparition   his marriage vows

were just a hollow chant
and what I took to be my bridegroom
was just a man prancing.

My husband has not touched me
since the wedding
he hasn't called me by my name.

I return to my father's house
still a virgin   my hair will turn grey
I will never have a child in my belly.

Spellbound

The first time I saw Shabtai Zvi
it was a warm summer day
hot sticky air hung motionless
in the cave of Machpelah.

He was swaying in a breeze
of prayer   eyes turned upwards
the way a child follows a kite
rise into the clouds.

People gathered in the cave
men women children spellbound.
A man in a white kaftan sighed
      Shabtai pronounced the sacred name of God.

I couldn't take my eyes off him
couldn't move.
I heard him singing   his voice
hummed in my mouth.

Abject

His hands tied to a post   he is bent forward
thirty nine lashes   with a leather thong.

His back on fire   his throat closing
he won't make a sound.

A crowd gathers   men and women
shaking   some praying   children crying.

They see his blisters   blue and black
and know it is to teach them a lesson.

And the blows keep coming drop
by drop of pain   tear his skin apart.

Someone counts out loud each stroke
חמש שש שבע שמונה   ... up to forty.

And then it's over   he staggers to his feet
and turns his red-hot face to the crowd

where it ignites the air with an afterglow
of heavenly flame.

Saturn

Thirty nine strokes / barbaric don't you think Shekhina / actually it's forty but the Talmud prescribes one less in case someone makes a mistake in counting / so what has he done to deserve it / staged a wedding ceremony / married himself to his beloved Torah scroll / invited all the rabbis to the banquet / must have been hilarious / not quite / they are afraid some new sect is fermenting in his brain / still it's just a harmless prank / don't you think / you always had a soft spot for him Lilith / yeah well / I think it's all to do with Saturn / even his name is telling / שבתאי [Shabtai] = Saturn / so what / it's melancholic / draws the soul to the inner world / who says / Walter Benjamin / he says it's the planet of utmost knowledge and prophecy / what does he know he isn't an astrologer is he / no but he was born under the sign of Saturn / so is he messianic too / not sure but he writes a lot about saturnines / like Proust or Kafka / oh please don't start me on Kafka right now /

Banished

Fool or deviant   he is banished
his city walking away

home   harbour   wives   dissolve
into hazy flecks on a vanishing point

a sudden sundown sinks into nightfall
dozy shadows crawl along the road
dark horizon closing in
a winged dragon at the edge of the world
is reaching out for him

sounds gather in his throat   rising
into a song   he sings to himself
the way a boy   eyes shut tight
will sing to scare away the dark

> *Esta noche mis kavalyeros*
> *durmi kon una donzella*
> *ke en los dias de mis dias*
> *no topi otra komo eya*
> *Meliselda tiene por nombre*
> *Meliselda galana i bella*
> *a la abashada de un rio*
> *i a la suvida de un varo*
> *enkontri kon Meliselda*
> *la ija del Imperante*
> *ke venia de los banios*
> *de los banios de la mare*

in early morning light   the sea a gleaming froth
colour begins   horizon stretches out empty   he steps in.

Wife to be

She tells of Cossacks on horseback
    galloping through the streets

broken houses burning with red tongues
    bodies flung to the ground

in this version her legs are trapped
    under a wall *I don't want to die* she gasps

a drawn-out dog howl answers
    awooo awooooo.

She is eight   an orphan taken to a convent
    to become a bride of Christ

on her knees behind latticed iron grates
    she is crying for her father

she tells how father entered her dream
    while the world was wrapped in sleep

how he dragged her through the window
    lifting her above the clouds

all the while new stories flutter
        and soar with each retelling.

Crashlanding

Did I tell you Sarah crashlanded in India / oh no it was in Persia among gravestones stripped naked an angel gave her a coat of skin / I don't get it Lilith / well it was lowered from heaven / hmmm / made by Eve six thousand years ago I read it in *Heavenly News* / really they say the angel promised her she'll be the bride of the new Messiah say angels can see the future / I still don't get it / sorry

Maidservant

Some days as I'm cleaning the skillets
I think of the time we worked in Livorno,
like how she loved polishing the silver

or when she told us how she was kidnapped
to be married to a wealthy gentile.
One time she said she was going to Jerusalem

to marry the messiah. We all giggled
and Solomon the apprentice hissed
in my ear
> *the whore will marry the Messiah*
> *che ridicolo!*

Sometimes I think if only I had gone with her
after Solomon pushed me up against the wall
perhaps I too could have become a bride.

Wedding

Cairo, April 1664

Dear Esther,

I remember fondly the time we worked
together in Livorno but the people here
treat me with much respect.
a famous rabbi asked me to prophesy his future
which I delivered with great finesse
I told him the roots of his soul
trace back to the noble sages of the past
you can imagine he was well pleased.

When I first met my bridegroom
he gave me a ring as a token of betrothal
but he seemed a bit apprehensive
as if facing turbulence at sea
I haven't yet discovered what troubles him
but trust me I will.

The day before the wedding I was taken
by three women to immerse myself in the mikveh
strip naked   scrub every surface – skin nails
hair – all that is in touch with the outside world
all of me drawn into the water three times.

And when it was over I was perfumed
with rose water and the women were singing
> *que peinaba sus cabellos con un peine de marfil*

and I felt as if I were breathing for the first time.

Next I must tell you about the wedding
you have never seen anything like this
for our host is Raphael Joseph Chelebi,
the leader of Egypt's Jewish community.
I wore a satin dress trimmed with lace
my husband a royal blue damask coat
and the houseboy served a most delicious
tavola di dolci to divert the evil demons
from casting a spell.

It is almost a month since the wedding
but my husband has not touched me once
last week I brushed my fingers against his arm
ever so lightly   you should have seen
how he turned pale   recoiled
as if he had been fondled by the demon Lilith.

I am beginning to think he doesn't know
what to do with a woman
his friends likewise
lower their gaze when they see me
they spend days and nights studying
it seems to me what they need is some practice.

One day soon I'll arrange for you to join me
they need women like us to teach them
for now I am enclosing an embroidered
silk handkerchief as a token of my friendship.

Messiah on the edge

And then it was darkness
       despite the prayers   the supplications
             the fasting   the flogging   the wedding
                   the confessions and the atonement of sins
                          there was no more illumination.

Bruised   deserted   withered
as if Saturn had cast its dark shadow on earth
he felt sick in his soul
the flame in his heart withered.

Somehow he made it to Gaza
for he had heard of the learned rabbi Nathan
a celebrated doctor of souls who knew
the secrets of every heart and prescribed
a tikkun for all manner of affliction.

And once he arrived it was a pandemonium
a throng of sinners jostling for restoration
but when Nathan and Shabtai eyed each other
something clicked into place.

Why are you here asked the rabbi
and fell to his knees trembling
you need no mending   you have risen to perfection.
Then they heard the sound of trumpets
and a roar from heaven
declaring *Shabtai Zvi is king Messiah.*

Unbridle my heart

Suddenly in the dark of night
my lips parched
my fingers
    veins of autumn leaves
crumbling to the touch

I turned backwards   came across
a wandering soul
      lost in a whirl of turbulence

and I know not how he
 lodged
    in the curve of my chest
unbridled my heart

I will pray to him and fast
   my passion will follow his command

and I saw the face of the east gather pink
until darkness
   was cut
     and before me
        it was light.

Performance

I tell you Lilith it was truly an amazing performance at an all-night vigil with the rabbis of Gaza Nathan rising unsteady on his feet as if sleepwalking   begins swaying   shaking all over in a trance   Nathan taking off his clothes – coat   trousers   shirt down to his underwear Nathan falling flat on the ground like a corpse / spooky don't you think Shekhina / gets even spookier just as the rabbis put a white cloth on his face as you do for the dead they   heard   a   voice   from underneath *take care of my beloved son, my Messiah Shabtai Zvi and of Nathan his prophet* / well it could have been just a conjuring trick / maybe but it was brilliant / do you really believe the Messiah is here with us / well just watch how the whole of Gaza goes wild   and Nathan the great impresario issues press releases announcing the glad tidings /

...

ok I am truly impressed but why did he take off his clothes / well it could have been a secret message / how come / do you remember when we read the story of King David dancing naked in front of the holy ark   remember the teacher told us there is nothing to be ashamed   of before god

well it is that same King David who cried   *how wondrous has thy love been to me surpassing the love of women* / so you think something is going on between Nathan and Shabtai / could be / anyway the teacher didn't explain what *surpassing* means.

On the road

No fool or deviant   the banished returns as Messiah
his city dancing towards him
ship masts   harbour   home   emerge
from hazy flecks on a vanishing point
amid the dazzle of glare and glitter at sundown

> *Meliselda galana i bella ...*
> *los sus kaveyikos ruvios*
> *paresen sirma de labrare*

low in the eastern sky a comet appears
                before a golden light at dawn

the city opens its gates   he steps in.

Procession

Halfway through slitting the hen's neck
the bird still in my hand thrashing about
I heard my wife call and rushed to the porch.

Outside neighbours and strangers surged forward
like a brood of chickens at feeding time
to glimpse the Messiah's procession –

    a boy is carrying a silver bowl laden with sweets
        two men hold vases of lilies and roses
            a rabbi parades Shabtai's inlaid ivory comb
                two rabbis holding the hem of his robe.

And then   incredible!
the Messiah strides past my house
waving his silver-plated fan over my head
as if brushing away layers of sorrow and pain.

Banquet

On Monday there was a great rejoicing as the Scroll of the Law was taken from the Ark. Shabtai sang all kinds of songs, also Christian songs in the vernacular, saying that there was a mystery hidden in these impure songs. He also declared *this day is my Sabbath day*.

At night he held a banquet and the people went to kiss his feet. To all of them he distributed money and candies, and he commanded all, Jews and gentiles alike, to utter the Ineffable Name. One gentile admitted that at Shabtai's persistent demand he had three times said it.

Even the Turks were talking about the Messiah, though no one ever saw a miracle, not even a natural sign. But many unlettered men and women experienced all manner of convulsions and prophesied and exclaimed, *Shabtai Zvi is the king of Israel!*

Unbeliever

Friday afternoon. A crowd gathers
outside my house. Then the first stone.
And another. A cloudburst of stones.
Windows crack.
> *Stone the infidel* the mob yells.
> I barricade the house.
> We slump down in the cellar.
> Crowd about to break in.

Friday sunset. Sabbath's service
begins. Crowd disperses.

Sabbath. I walk to the synagogue
for morning prayers. Shabtai sends
a messenger to the elders.
> *Eject the infidel from the synagogue*
> he demands.
> Elders refuse. Lock the gates.

The mob again. A throng of followers
in a frenzy. Shabtai at the head
axe in hand. A torrent of blows rains down
in a flurry of rage. Gates break open.
Crowd storms in.
> *Capture the infidel* they scream.
> In haste I climb out the window.
> Escape over the roof.

Heartbeat racing. I run like never before.
Rushing home.
My two daughters still in the cellar. Safe.

Rage

Outrageous / smashed the door of the synagogue with an axe / on the Sabbath / can you believe it / barged in / his followers in tow / hundreds of them / a gang of stormtroopers / come on he isn't some Darth Vader / well you should have seen his rage / a gaping red mouth filled with dizzy whirls of insults lashed out at the rabbis / threatened to throw them out of the synagogue / ironic isn't it / the very same rabbis who banished him years ago / so you say is it about revenge / maybe / I think it really got into him / the thrill of wielding power / out to torment his opponents / until they submit / sad / to see the chief rabbi make a public about-face / honour the newly declared king / well people do change their minds / don't they /

Blessed

Smyrna, December 1665

Dear Esther,

At last. I thought it would never happen.
It took almost two years for a message
from heaven to arrive   commanding us
to consummate our marriage.
He was nervous   a bit clumsy
needed my hand to ignite the spark.
I sensed his body tense up   his heartbeat quicken
after ten minutes of moan and surge
red and sweaty
a sudden swell unlocked the floodgate.

Do I love him? For sure we are in it together
a finger-prick drop of blood on a white sheet
(please don't laugh) my virginity
on public display a cause for rejoicing.
Men and women dance together
women called to read the Torah on Sabbath.
Imagine my husband in the synagogue
declaring *I have come to make you women
free and happy* (people say he's under my spell
I smile serenely).

Blessed days upon us. Torchlight processions
parade through the city calling
        long live the Messiah king.
Visitors from distant lands
wait for days to be admitted to our royal residence.

I am sending my servant Jacob to fetch you.
He can be trusted to bring you safely to Smyrna
to become my lady-in-waiting.

Messiah in love

He has discovered something most wonderful.
So much unknown, rich and mystifying.
True happiness in the folds of her flesh.

A gaze to reach his heart. Is this what love is?
To let her hold him, steer his life.
She is with him to face a yearnful crowd.

A kiss

I'm bored Lilith / why what's up / had enough of my goody-two-shoes image   I'd love to be more naughty   wear an amazing dress   a frothy pink *Killing Eve* item   or a sleek little black outfit like yours / oh I see you're a bit jealous when I have fun   I tell you sometimes it's amusing to be horrid but really   I'm fed up with my demons   forever playing dirty tricks   leading people astray you know what wish I could be more worthy like you /
I suppose we can't break free of our destiny always hover watch   eavesdrop   telling other people's stories /   yes just being nosey   but truly I'd love to be part of their stories   like being in love with a human /   me too sometimes I think how happy humans must be   to smell to embrace to kiss / yes but what about their dirty laundry their grief and pain   surely you don't fancy death /
   still what about a kiss /

Miracles

Every day people talked about miracles
on Monday Aaron the tailor saw fire shoot out
of Shabtai's mouth
and set the Qadi's beard alight

on Tuesday Mordechai the baker swore
the heavens opened up at dawn
and he saw Shabtai at the blazing gateway
wearing a mighty crown

yesterday a spinster from Galata said
an angel holding a flaming sword
revealed to her the Messiah had come
and would soon appear on the shores of the Jordan

last night I found my two daughters
foaming at the mouth in a fit of ecstasy
   calling out
        crown crown   Shabtai Zvi
           sits on an exalted throne in heaven

a miracle in my own house
the whole world seemed out of joint
that sense of sinking through mud

surrender or your daughters are lost to you
so I bit my tongue and said
   Shabtai Zvi is the true Messiah

Devotion

At first it was painless. I got up at midnight
to recite the daily devotion and confessed my sins
immersed in a ritual bath so crowded it was nearly
impossible to enter: *for whoever is not clothed
with the breastplate of repentance will suffer
great tribulations*, proclaimed our prophet Nathan.

Eager to hasten the advent of the Messiah
I refined the prescribed bodily mortifications:
I rolled downhill naked in a blizzard of snow,
or threw myself into the frozen winter sea.

Gripped by desire for eternal salvation
some days I stripped naked, wrapped my body
in thorns and nettles, my skin
crisscross-scratched to mark my penitence
for vanity, misdeeds and ill-gotten gains.

I disposed of my business to provide for the needy.
No longer rich or poor, miser or destitute,
all will be swept away when Saturn reaches
its highest point in the sky
and bathes the earth in boundless light.

Wager

From *The Dairy of Samuel Pepys*

I have heard once or twice already, of a Jew in town, that in the name of the rest do offer to give any man £10 to be paid £100, if a certain person now at Smyrna be within these two years honoured by all the Princes of the East, and particularly the grand Signor as the King of the world, in the same manner we do the King of England here, and that this man is the true Messiah. One named a friend of his that had received ten pieces in gold upon this score, and says that the Jew hath disposed of £1100 in this manner, which is very strange; and certainly this year of 1666 will be a year of great action; but what the consequences of it will be, God knows.

Soup

Ice drizzle is blowing up the frozen Elbe. My daughter's lips
are blue. I wrap a woollen shawl over her shoulders.
Yesterday I sold 300 ounces of assorted seed pearls
for a good profit. Reached an agreement with creditors.

Aunt Bela brings a basket of beetroot from the market
merciful God, she cries, *the king Messiah proclaimed!*
She tells of a letter from Smyrna. Outbursts of joy
in the synagogue. Young and old in finest clothes
dancing to the beating of drums.
Aunt Bela is breathless, delirious. My daughter
is still freezing. I chop beetroot, carrot and onions
for a steaming soup at dinner time.

Yearning

Baffling innit / what / how people can be so gullible / come on Lilith, a bit of empathy wouldn't go amiss / you mean show some concern / yes, imagine the suffering, the pogroms, the pain of exile, the yearning for deliverance / so it's like dreaming of utopia / maybe but utopia actually means no-place / how do you know / Thomas More invented it but I think it was satirical and frankly I don't fancy his utopia that much / I thought utopia was dead / well she hibernates for years and years, then bursts out with a fury, flaps, spins, then hides again / how poetic, so you think this messiah-craze will end badly / not sure, the prognosis isn't too good / who says / Walter Benjamin says even if the messiah does turn up one day nothing much would change / a bit pessimistic innit / yes but there is always hope, remember old Vladimir and Estragon / well they're still waiting

Birth pangs

The morning is bright and airy. Another letter arrives.
Messiah to be crowned by the Sultan. Father-in-law
packs two barrels of food slow to perish –
peas, smoked meat, dried fruits.
The good man prepares to sail to the Holy Land
through a storm-tossed, angry sea.
Birth pangs of the Messiah, he says.

Splendid

Gallipoli, July 1666

Dear Esther,

It's hard to imagine the love and devotion
of believers and well wishers
who arrive with splendid gifts,
like the lustrous heirloom carpets
presented by the envoi from Kurdistan,
the bejewelled silver vessels
made by Heshel Soref,
the renowned silversmith of Vilna,
or my husband's most favourite,
the deep red damask silk robe
depicting a lion embroidered
with gold metal threads,
sent by worshippers from Podolia.

Yet my husband seemed anxious, unsettled,
and his sleeplessness worried me.
I'd lie awake and listen to him shuffling
listless in the dark.
He seemed terrified of sleep.

What is this affliction? I asked a visiting rabbi.
Melancholia, he said. He told me the remedy
advised by the famous physician Maimonides
is music and dance, or a walk in the garden
watching pretty flowers or shapely women.

I invited a group of Turkish dancing-boys
accompanied by a band of musicians
to perform for my husband and his guests.
I taught the most beautiful girls how to walk
through the garden, hips swaying gently,
a twinkle in the eye, with just a hint of a smile.

It worked like a dream. Imagine my husband
bewitched by the curve of a breast outlined
through a silky dress, his eyes crawling over
a raised armpit, uplifting his spirit to the height
of ecstasy. Eager, unruly, he swaggers
like a boy, insatiate, demands seventy virgins.

I think it's a bit of bravado to make up
for missed pleasures in the past,
but he's so full of his fire now,
throwing all caution to the wind.
Be careful, I tell him, *not to provoke
the unbelievers.*
He seems not to understand
how these things work.

Politics

So the Messiah survived a shipwreck / well just about / got a real battering / those monster waves / you know the Hellespont in winter / so what was he doing there / he was called by God to Constantinople / what for / to remove the Sultan's crown and place it on his own head / that's crazy / not really he followed the script of Nathan's prophecy / ah Nathan haven't heard from him for a while / well he is still in Gaza prophesying / rumour has it he doesn't like queen Sarah that much /
why's that / dunno, that poet says she's a witch practising her dark arts in the heat of night / I think Nathan is envious that the Messiah truly loves his wife / maybe but what happened to the Messiah / he was arrested at sea / oh that's horrible / I read it in *Heavenly News* they say he was brought ashore in chains and hit by the guards / I don't believe it I think the authorities know that he has many secret followers among the Turks too / so you say they are afraid to upset them / Well, that's just politics, isn't it

Pilgrim

How blessed I felt to join the pilgrims
from the ends of the earth arriving to pay homage
to our king Messiah and his noble countenance.

How glorious it is to behold his majesty
wearing a regal red robe adorned with sparkling
golden-tasselled threads.

How delightful it is to glimpse the bare ankle
of a dazzling maiden strolling gently
in our master's garden.

How can it be right, I asked our king, *for it is a sin
to look at even the small finger of a woman?*

Blessed is he who permits that which is forbidden,
he said, revealing the great mystery
how he has intercourse with beautiful virgins
without deflowering them.

My lord and king, I said, *may I stay a servant
at your court, for I have yet so much to learn.*

Upon which, rising to his feet, our king
began to sing in a mighty voice, eyes raised to heaven,
as if ascending to the celestial paradise.

Gossip

In the port and in the synagogues
in the sweaty throng of the bazaar
who has not heard the latest gossip

> *The Messiah has persuaded a young man*
> *to enter Queen Sarah's room,*
> *a voice*
> *whispers in my ear,*
> *he fled when she approached him.*

It is hard for the boy, I told Shabtai,
he is shocked and distressed
for he is respectful, and only wanted
to pay homage to the queen.

If only he had done her will, Shabtai said,
he would have performed a great tikkun.
The other boys didn't run away, he said.

Omen

Gallipoli, September 1666

Dear Esther,

It was really creepy, this distinguished rabbi
from Poland, plump, broad-shouldered,
with a grey beard silvered at the temples.
I felt a shudder through my body,
like seeing
my father's ghost visiting my husband.

I watched them argue. *It is written,*
the rabbi insisted, *the war of Gog and Magog
must take place before
the coming of the messiah.*
All day he listed further signs and omens
to prove that Shabtai is a false messiah.

I could see my husband was panicking,
leafing through book after book,
desperate
for proof of his claims to be the Messiah,
each one rejected by the visiting rabbi
as vanity
and ignorance of the correct interpretation.

You wouldn't believe it! For three days and nights
they carried on squabbling as if they were
two drunkards picking a fight in the tavern
with no end in sight,
until the visiting rabbi, in a furious outburst,
called Shabtai a traitor.

I am confused, my husband is dedicated
to saving his people,
and he is about to be crowned by the Sultan.
And yet maybe the ghost of my father is an omen.

Conversion

Did you hear that? The disgruntled rabbi from Poland complained to the Sultan / really what about / he said that Shabtai is a lewd person who corrupts the minds of the Jews / disgusting what a snitch couldn't they just fight it out between themselves / well they didn't and next day Shabtai was taken to the Sultan's court to stand trial for treason / unbelievable I just missed this story / how come this is truly sensational / I was distracted fantasising what it's like to kiss a human / anyway Shabtai renounced his claims to the messianic title said he is just a poor rabbi with no special privilege or virtue / what a coward his followers must have been shocked / not really they think it was a cunning plot in any case the Sultan offered Shabtai a choice – convert to Islam or die impaled on a stake at the Gate of the Seraglio / blimey what a choice / actually it is a no brainer particularly with the promise of an honorary post and a royal pension / come on Lilith don't be so cynical maybe he genuinely believes this is ordained by God / bizarre don't you think –

A Jewish messiah becomes Aziz Mehmet Effendi an honorary keeper of the palace gates / well at least he didn't have to get circumcised.

Obedience

What is obedience? *A wife is required*
to obey her husband,
for he is her gateway to paradise,
says the Sultan's mother who instructs me
in the ways of Islam.

I am now Fatima Kadin, a dutiful wife
who follows her husband's command.
You must recite the Shahadah with genuine
conviction, says the Sultan's mother.

I remember how my father was murdered
for refusing to convert, how I sang
the matins in the convent chapel,
pretending
to be a Christian girl.

I think of Queen Esther who concealed
her Jewish origins from King Ahasuerus
to bring salvation to her people.
Perhaps my husband too is on a mission,
a divine secret to be revealed in the fullness of time.

1666

Annus mirabilis, writes John Dryden, *angels
drew wide the curtains of the skies*. Robert Hooke
observes shadows cast by the rings of Saturn
with a 60-foot telescope. Young Isaac Newton
sits under a tree, the apple about to fall.
In the spring the swallows return.

The Ottoman army departs for the bloodiest Siege
of Candia. There are rumours that the Venetians
prepare to lift the siege by infecting the Ottomans
with plague. At the première of *Le Misanthrope*
in Paris the critics are unimpressed
by the harangues and moral preaching.
In London the theatres are shut.

In June the Dutch fleet moves off Galloper Sand
towards the channel. Dutch fireships set alight
the English ship *Resolution*. Two months
later Samuel Pepys is watching
a most horrid malicious bloody flame
engulfing the streets.
It made me weep to see it, he writes.
Dutch citizens are accused of starting the fire.
In September Shabtai Zvi converts to Islam.

In the autumn there are several sightings
of swallows under water.
The Royal Society of London concludes
that swallows do not travel south for winter.
It is most certain they hibernate in ponds, like frogs.
Annus mirabilis, writes Fatima Kadin to Esther Levy,
I can feel baby flutters in my belly.

Wind

Gloomy, cold and wet. Father-in-law
unpacks his barrels, exhausted.
His dream of redemption is shattered.

How we have waited! Rumours
were stirred to a glowing blaze,
shaking loose hushed dreams.
We said so many prayers,
gave away our possessions to charity,
laid bare
our bodies and souls to penitence
and mortification.

We were like a woman on a birthing stool
who, after long labour and sore pains,
expects to rejoice in the birth of a child,
yet finds it is nothing but wind.

Mysteries

Every day people talk about mysteries
Aaron the tailor says Shabtai didn't convert
that in fact it was the Sultan who embraced him
and set the royal crown on his head.

Mordechai the baker swears the conversion
is part of a divine plan
that Shabtai has entered the evil forces
of the qlippot in order to subdue them.

The spinster from Galata claims
it is not he himself who has converted
but a shadow. The real Shabtai
rose into the sky and has disappeared.

Last night I found my two daughters
whirling barefoot in a trance
   singing
> *oh, my beloved's gone from me*
> *God's chosen one, Shabtai Zvi*
> *though fallen low and suffering hard*
> *yet he is closest to my heart*

the whole world is out of joint
that sense of sinking through mud.

A crooked pathway

At the pre-dawn hour, the time of divine favour
he spoke the language of dreams –
how he fell into a deep pit and couldn't get out,
how he saw his father and mother
standing above by the edge, how they threw down
a rope and pulled him out of the pit.

At sunrise I saw him in the Portuguese synagogue
chanting the *shacharit* prayers in a mellow tune.
I stood there petrified, watching him perform
the *namaz*, bowing and rising in supplication.
At the end of the service he read from the Qur'an
commanding his followers to put on the turban.

How blessed I felt to behold our King's radiance,
yet I prayed he would spare me the agony
of embracing Islam. I knew I would have obeyed
if our beloved messiah required me to descend
with him into the realm of the qlippot to lift
the holy sparks that had fallen to the great abyss.

I was with him when his light was eclipsed,
shut away in the power of the serpents
until in his suffering he inclined to heresy,
his faith a single hair's breadth from extinction,
but when his illumination returned
not even a hair's breadth of doubt remained.

When we rabbis saw his light restored, we fanned
him with a fan, like slaves to their master.
His muddled soul may lead us to misfortune,
yet the sparks he ignited will guide us
through the crooked pathway to the gates
of divine revelation.

Betrayal

Unbelievable performing the *namaz* in the synagogue truly muddled / actually I think he is trying to blend the two religions together quite revolutionary really spiritual freedom just think of Spinoza / yeah well both get excommunicated / and both challenge the fossilised beliefs of the old world / still Spinoza is rational Shabtai is hot-headed remember the live fish in the cradle / yeah and sometimes he is really nasty like persecuting the unbelievers for refusing to have faith in him / well he is a bit mad like now he is divorcing Sarah / that's crazy I think she is beautiful and clever / and she wholeheartedly believes in his messianic destiny / so what's got into him all of a sudden / he says she is like leprosy which according to the Talmud is a valid ground for divorce / you forget he is a Muslim now / well that's simple – a man does not need to state the grounds for divorce / anyway I suspect he plotted the whole thing with Nathan / sounds true Nathan never liked her / now he spreads rumours that Sarah persecutes her husband calls her

a snake   says she tried to poison
Shabtai twice in short he's plain
beastly / both of them actually/
typical innit   same old story
woman/snake/temptress/fall   etc.
as Milton says *those innumerable
disturbances on Earth through
female snares* / I can't believe it
did Milton really say this / well he
made Adam speak it / all the same
to me but what happened to Sarah
/ not even a Wikipedia entry about
her / frankly I am fed up I no
longer want to tell this Messiah's
story / that's it   from now on we
are just telling Sarah's story.

Miraculous

Smyrna, April 1668

Dear Esther,

Please forgive me for not writing to you until now.
What a turbulent time I have had.
You might have heard my husband divorced me.
He said I was a snake, trying to poison him.
I believe it was all Nathan's idea.
Just like that – pack my bags and leave.

You can imagine how hurt I felt.
Discarded, betrayed, left alone in the world.
I saw my life slipping away in a cloud of gravel dust.
I was lost, with only the faint voice
of my dead father ticking inside my brain:
hold your head high daughter
show them what you are made of.
Return to Smyrna, urged the voice,
make a different version of your life.

So here I am again, invited to reside
with the chief magistrate's widow
and treated with kindness and respect.
People remember me. They call me
señora profetisa, ask me to read their palms,
or the tarot cards.
Will I be allowed to marry my true love?
they ask, or, *will my husband divorce me*
for denying his conjugal rights?
will there ever be a messiah for women?

It's up to us women to get together, I tell them
redeem ourselves from oppression and injustice,
and *yes, every righteous woman can become*
the saviour of her people.
For added gravity and poise I sometimes wear
the embroidered red damask silk robe,
which, I confess, I have taken from my husband's
coffer as my illicit parting gift.

A visiting scholar from Jerusalem said
I remind him of the Biblical prophetess Miriam.
I felt so moved – I imagined myself
as Miriam leading the Israelite women
with song and dance to celebrate
their deliverance from slavery in Egypt.

Is this a letter with a happy ending? you may ask.
Well, the learned man from Jerusalem said
that God punished Miriam with a horrible
affliction for her sin of pride.
But after seven days God forgave her
and she endowed the Israelites
with a miraculous well named after her
that provided fresh water
during their years of wandering in the desert.

Notes

Shabtai Zvi – spelling varies in different translations. I use Shabtai Zvi which is nearer to contemporary Hebrew pronunciation.

A bit of an oddball – after Anne Carson.

Un poco loco – a bit crazy.

Meliselda – Ladino (*Judeoespañol*): This night my cavaliers / I slept with a maiden / whose equal I have never met / in the best years of my life / Meliselda is her name, / Meliselda elegant and beautiful / along the course of a river / and the slope of a hill / I met Meliselda /daughter of the Emperor / who came to bathe herself / in the waters of the sea.
Meliselda, a popular Judeo-Spanish romansa, was Shabtai Zvi's favourite song, later incorporated into the Sabbatean liturgy.

Tikkun – mending. In the Kabbalah restoring the damaged world into its primordial wholeness.

Mikveh – a Jewish ritual bath.

Que peinaba sus cabellos… – Ladino: who is combing her hair with an ivory comb.

Qlippot – 'shells' or 'husks' which conceal holiness, like a peel concealing the fruit within. In the Kaballah they are considered as a representation of evil or impure spiritual forces.

Shahadah – the Muslim declaration of faith and the first Pillar of Islam.

Shacharit – Jewish morning prayer.

Namaz – Muslim prayer.

Sources

Latham, R., & Matthews, W. (1976). The Diary of Samuel Pepys: a new and complete transcription. Berkeley.

The poetry was informed by a great deal of background reading with particualr thanks to the following texts:

Scholem, G. (1973). Sabbatai Sevi: The Mystical Messiah, 1626-1676. (Princeton UP).

Werses, S. (2001). 'Meliselda Coming up from the Bath', *Pe'amim* (2000/2001): 75–97. (article in Hebrew)